Psyche and the hurricane

Psyche and the hurricane

Michèle Roberts

First published in Great Britain in 1991
by Methuen London,
Michelin House, 81 Fulham Road, London sw3 6rb

Copyright © 1991 Michèle Roberts
The author has asserted her moral rights

isbn 0 413 65020 0
A CIP catalogue record for this book
is available from the British Library

Printed and bound in Great Britain
by Cox & Wyman Ltd, Reading, Berks.

for Jackie

Methuen

Some of these poems have previously
appeared in the following periodicals:
Critical Quarterly, Tampa Review,
So This Is Love, First and Always,
Jacaranda Review, Bête Noire,
Arvon International Poetry Competition 1987 anthology.

Thanks to Judith Kazantzis and Sarah Maguire
for reading and criticising the manuscript.
Thanks to John Osborne and all at *Bête Noire*.
Thanks to Geoffrey Strachan and Louise Moore
of Methuen.

Contents

Psyche and the hurricane

The Alps are a college of grandmothers in white caps. Massed
profiles rear up, as pure
as nuns'.

They dandle only the air
on their scalloped laps.
Clouds infiltrate
their knees' blue valleys.

Closer, they are all
mouth: discussing
the clatter of pilots out of tin
carrycots onto these ridged tips
that snap them up, teeth
needling the lovely boys, tongues
sucking the gristle off bones.

You could easily lose your heart
to these bad grannies:
they are so possessive!

They'll cherish
the flesh of businessmen
better than any hostess, these
lipsmacking sisters; they'll
teach young wives and other
survivors how to carve up
the sun-dried dead, and eat.

We scuttle past.
Now we're only a glint
in their turquoise eye.

Patience is their vocation.

praise blue

Blue torrent of plastic crates
under the market stalls
of Sant' Ambrogio.

Blue swollen and tight
as aubergine skins: rain
of shiny truncheons.

Blue bursts in my mouth:
juice avalanche of trays
of muscat grapes.

Blue mountain of dusky plums
patched with black. Sweet bruises
fat as eggs.

Blue shoots off in all directions:
violet tips of cream turnips
mauve asters and radicchio frills.

My blue cotton dress with white
spots, my navy espadrilles
let me fit in.

The sky wraps it up.
Ink shadows under the eaves
at noon. I dissolve in blue

with just one cigarette
called MS Blu
its blue steam writhing.

The green glass throats of the wine
bottles moisten and perspire.

Waiters fastidious as priests
scoop up crumbs with tongs
off the white cloth.
Even the plates wear collars.

How these old men fret and strut
waggling their chicken necks.
They nip and peck in polite
spite, shriek discreetly
jostling for first strike.

The senator's trussed
in a silk suit
basted with cologne, his shirt-front
larded with pearl studs.
His eyelashes bat like a movie star's.
His hands are javelins and fans.

Three wives are strategically placed
as condiments, supposed
to pepper these
cross spouses with kind looks
spice them back into niceness.

What they need
is to be gagged with their napkins.

I shut my mouth, biting on
grilled aubergines'
delicious flesh and crackly
blackened skin.
It slips down easily.

Il barone rampante

On the eve of the New Year feast
an army of amazon cooks
tackles his kitchen.

The dead salmon winks
from its pastry bier.
He retreats
from the stripped prawns
the boiling cauldrons of oil
stalks out
with rucksack and alpenstock.

Up through the snowy woods
he plots his complex way
unmapped, unmarked.
The man of the mountains
puts together a white
jigsaw with black cracks.

Warnings drip from the rocks.
The mountain man
who hides in the tops
of trees and
licks snow off bushes
has a tongue of ice.

His boots yelp over snow.
The dark jaw of the cave
juts like his when he mutters:
'Tell her to give me *sa chose.*'

The grotto's his true
house: bed of beech
leaves, table and chair
carried here on his back
his bag of poems.

He curls between stone lips
starving. The mountain
gulps him in.
One day he will never come out.

for Paula, mourning

The Museo Civico garden
is a coffin of snow.
Fresh scent of bitter privet.
The fountain halts.

Grief buckles itself onto you
like a new winter coat.
Sono una ragazza distrutta
you tell me. Your skin
topples away. Life
cuts you up
like a raw potato.

You hold a second funeral
alone, filling the room
with candles and flowers
on New Year's Eve
drinking champagne
from the best crystal glass.

Paula, museum-keeper
you catalogue the smell of loss
in corridors, in letters. You
exhibit absence. You
list the many categories
of worldly joy.
Kneeling to dust the floor
the way your mother did
you acquire
her gestures.

Paula, curator of memories
keeper of your parents' house
I tell you
your mother
will rise inside you
strongly as the moon.

The road to Trento
(for Sarah giving birth)

White dashes. White dots.
Two white strokes:
a pine tree; a roof.

White pockmarks and scars
on beech trunks. White Vs
on what must be mountains.

Snow, sifted exactly, catches
all horizontals, out-
lines them. White
blocked onto white.

Waves and flurries
of frost
repeat, repeat.
Branches
fling up and out
like quivering wires.

We force ourselves
gently
through the cold pass

like your child
toboganning on
your slope
the world turning
itself inside out

the world
turning around
the world
bearing down.

We come down
into the valley
of castles and vineyards
and small white fields
combed with a black comb.

The fruit trees are ice.
I hear your great shout.

A weekend in the Dolomites

The car sucks up the road:
kilometres tick by, metallic
round as a stop-
watch, a measuring tape.

The sky scribbles an alphabet
of falling stars.
Foreign. Incomprehensible.
We're rapt as ants
under a black tin colander
with silvery holes.

Ear to the bedhead's
cathedral door:
people crawl between
other, invisible walls.

Through scorched-linen
curtains, the cold
breath of the mountains
gets hold of me
mouth open, closing on
nothing.

The woods smell of
mushrooms and rot.
Petals of light
lie on beech leaves.

Toadstools swell vicious
and yellow as jealousy.
Poison to husbands.

Some days I'm ugly
knowing no antidote.
My gaze terrorizes
a houseless fledgling
stubbled blue-black that
pants between tree-roots.

The green prairie
drops off the world. That's
flat. Just this itch
of insects on stilts of grass.

On the edge, waist tilted
over, I get a grip on
space. On the other side
of the void, peaks
fling up their chins.
I want to learn
how to be still
always falling.

The broken house

This is a house of tricks
flimsy as playing cards.
Patience. Griselda
does not complain.

The kitchen ceiling
clatters to the
terracotta floor. Plaster
cast-offs bear
criss-cross prints
of the woven cane lining
they clung to. Log
beams exposed: dead
forest, blackened
and split.
By noon we wear grey
stockings and grey perruques.

I withdraw like the furniture
to the next room: widows
massed close; untouchables
in transparent plastic veils.

The front window
sucks in scaffolding
bit by bit, bites on iron
with rope and tackle teeth.
The dust-choked house
throws up
over the sill. Buckets
of rubble squeal
to the street. No
stomach left. No heart.

Antonio and Giovanni
swap hammers in Calabrian
scrawl messages on stones.
They heave off the roof
in red handfuls. Huff
and puff: little pig
I shall blow your house down.
My arms are about the house
trying to hold it up: after
my great fall, who
will put me
together again?

Dirt
is a part of me. Pall
of plaster grains. Dust
to dust: I am already dying.

Down south, two women
put on black and
wait for letters.
My creased ghost
dangles in the wardrobe
and the post-box
cries for food, for
permission to exist
in duplicate: please tick
coniuge or *nubile*.

My sky torn down I'm
open-mouthed to the rain.
Pigeons shit in the bath.

No more floor: feet lost
in broken bricks I am
walled in air
bleak
as a marriage
I can't make
or mend.

Red stripes on casualties of conflict.
All full-timers welcome.

All marriages
should be loaded from the bottom drawer
working upwards
marked with your local bitter
maiden name if any.
This marriage is fitted with
an anti-tilt device.
Caution: dry riser inside.
Danger. Men working overtime.
Safety helmets are provided
for your protection
and must be worn.
Men working overhead
on these premises: as a rule
men are more muscular than women.
Women naturally burn off
their maiden names.

Doctors encourage women: build
up a bit more muscle, or multiples thereof
as safety holds when marriages are empty.

Men don't have the same pressure.
Sorry ladies! Doctors encourage women
in their heavy duty.
Please allow twenty-eight days
for delivery.
Love is sterilized
and supplied pre-packed.

The management regrets unmarried
card-carrying members only
make matters worse.

It is love.
It is war.
Between robots
in shorts and tights.
Already wounded, they're
swaddled in bandages
giant toddlers
with yellow skulls
who clomp on
faceless as spacemen
to the band's blare.

Two boxes. Two
toy armies, identical, all
holding their weapons up.
Now these knights
in soft armour spill
out, onto the hissing
ice, race to the mêlée
in a whirr of skates.
Hear the crowd's rude prayer, the
slick scrape of blades. See
the referee zip by in
black slacks, the sidesmen
chic stripey humbugs
skip up over the skimming puck.

In this war all's just: the
faked fall, trip-tricking, mixed
sticks and fibulas, locked
lobster claws. No time
to lip-read the wishes

mouthed behind perspex
visors: Hatje, Capone, Sweeney
Chiarelli, MacDonald, Bourbeau
must swish on to
victory, cracked
kneecaps, bearhugs.

So says the pretty lady in furs
and jewels and long suede gloves
who yawns over her programme, pouts
for popcorn, chocolate, chat

and who nuzzles her nose
uneasily
into her husband's cold ear.

Telephone calls in Boston
(performance piece for two male voices)

1

Hi, how *are* you?
Hi, how are *you*?
Hi. Hi, you. Hi, you.
What are you doing?
Are you? *Are* you? Anything?
Are you anything?
Anything doing? This afternoon?
What are you doing
this afternoon?
Do you wanna get *laid*?
Do you? *Do* you? I'll
do you. You'll do. I'll
get you laid. I'll
get you
this afternoon. Don't you
know who *this* is?
But you do fuck, don't you?
But you do fuck, don't you.
Don't you? But
you don't know. Don't you
wanna get laid?
But you do fuck don't you.

2

Listen, you.
You listen.
You shouldn't.
You shouldn't listen.

Listen, you shouldn't.
You listen: you shouldn't listen.
You should
hang up.
You shouldn't listen to his hang-ups.
Up. Shut up. Shut him up.
You should, shouldn't you?
You shouldn't talk back.
You shouldn't talk.
Shouldn't. You talk. You talk back. Talk?
Shouldn't talk back, you.
You only. Only you.
You only encourage him.

3

Shouldn't listen.
Shouldn't fuck.
Shouldn't talk back.

4

But you do fuck, don't you?
But you do fuck don't you.

Two news stories in The New York Times
(for Judith Kazantzis)

she screamed: save the children

What shall it profit an obstetrician
to gain the whole world in private practice
then lose fees
when he's forced to treat the poor?

in the brick apartment house
by the railroad tracks, thick
smoke, darkness, the red sparks

After years of educating these women
on the importance of pre-natal care
we have decided to withdraw provision.
Overheads and insurance have gone up

Johnetta Hodges, you are clothed in flames

out of all proportion with state reimbursement
so those on Medicaid shall never enter
this kingdom. Says Dr Robert Wilson:
we've always done it at a loss.

Johnetta Hodges turned, fled back
into the flames. From the fire
she brought the children out.
She delivered her son, and her sister's son
from the burning house. They crouch
in the motherless gutter, bawling
their eyes out on camera

I understand what you are saying about
conscience, says Dr Wilson: but I have to feed
my own family. A man's own
wife and children must come first.

Johnetta Hodges, you lie dead in the street.
You lie on the sidewalk in your dressing-gown
face on the cold stone, one arm flung out
ahead. Mary your mother leans apart from you
against the wall, bowed over
clutching her bellyful of grief

White women and children first
after white doctors. Save
the black children
if you have first saved money.

In Chicago, by the railroad tracks
Johnetta Hodges loves and burns

Coloured red

The swerve of
scarlet satin
tulips in their
death
dance: red
shining curves
flare up, fling out
then fall, flayed.

Red wine drunk
alone leaves bitter
grains settled
in the glass, a
cut-throat
rattle
of garnets.
Bite it. Crushed
splinters. Not
medicinal.

Red rot. Red
preparation
of a warm room
that must refuse guests.
Red desire, coiled
ready, snaps shut
on itself, wounded
by a cold spring.

Death, that red baby
tunnels through me.
My mouth aches
delivering
my red word.
There.
It is out now.

I'm living in the wrong house.

Stuck in the speechless lodgings
I hold my breath
to make the evenings pass
hearing the television
and the telephone
downstairs.

Blocked from the kitchen
by a foreign body
my hands
stitched into a thriller
keep trying
to hang up my apron
on invisible hooks.

Nobody knows the names
my best friends call me.
Nobody, politely
notices my eyes.

Neat in black linen
I smirk over drinks
at academics tight-
lipped as wallets.

My mouth kisses a cigarette
so as not to embarrass.
Paid mother, paid midwife
paid muse
to others' words.

I'm big with emptiness
as these winter fields
I pass on my way to work.

Just you and me now
I bellow to the polished coils
of broken flowerpots.

Through the mist
sunlight spreads itself
on the churned earth
cold and calm as milk.

Blue air
on the mane
of the hill

where fields dissolve
to lavender, a
blotting-paper sky.

Flat frieze
of elms, sharp
as a paper cut-out.

Thick strokes
of darkness.

Through the ink
tangle of trees
the moon struggles up
and spills out
free, a
sudden light-flood.

A bullock's invisible lips
close over grass. Hiss
of nettles. Tiny
swallows of rain
by plantains and docks.

Stars dangle, bright
yo-yos, over
earth, that mud baby.

In Holland Park
the houses yawn in pastels.
Pink ironed girls, plaits under boaters
are swept to school in Volvos
by clean fathers popping to the City.
Speechless *au pairs* and babies
push off to the park. Mothers
gulp gin
at elevenses
in cool tiled kitchens of Italian décor.

Outside each house
a man in blue
cap and jacket sits
bent over, wide-
legged on the pavement.
The stone seams burst apart:
urgent delivery
into his patient hands.
He clutches a bright snarl of colours:
fistfuls of spiralling current
jump in his lap, an electric bouquet.

Jollity sloshes along the patios
at dusk. Beasts roast on barbecues.
Fathers in sports shirts
spear cocktail onions. Mothers
give sloppy ice grins.

In the stitched-up street
the pavements bear traces
of fresh cement scars. The *au pairs*

blue as aerograms patrol
the nurseries. All thumbs
they spell today's vocabulary
the next explosion.

Driving to Hereford

Along the steep valley
the road with its quick
zigzag back
and forth
across the Wye
stitches up
old warring borders:
England/Wales.

But the river
breaks through
green grass-threads
like a birth, speaks
with its green mouth:
I come to separate
I come to divide.

Clouds bowl along
the top of the ridge:
white wave-splash
onto the beach of hills.

In the hospital
you stitched up the lips
of wounds. Then
hitch-hiked a ride
back, stuck
your lips to the car's
udder, and sucked.

The river flows on anyway
and the child looks up

from his book:
who is Charon?

Clouds, and the shadows of clouds
moving over the hills.

You held all your words
down. Swollen. Then you dived in.

Psyche, imprisoned in the paint, has
got free, and wields a bucket. White
vest against her golden
shoulders, white overalls rolled
about her waist, she caresses
her sisters' eyes with a wet sponge.

Return to that house of desire
made flesh. Re-vision it. Discard
the cradle of winds, all magical escorts.
Prefer to be engineer
locking your steps to the air
on scaffolding frames
clasped with rusty latches.

She stares at the dream. Level after level
of images falls past. She clambers up
four ladders of narrative
till she swings free
in the vault of darkness, the
silence between sentences.

She's equipped with a photo-map
topped by a plastic sheet she
marks with a Pentel pen. Knocking
at the plaster of the myth's crust
she listens for disturbances
below the surface.

Now she is close to the invisible god:
pressing her ear to a deep crack
she hears him breathing.

Leaning over him, daring and disobedient
she hoists her lamp, clips it
to a metal strut, switches
the beam of her love full on.

At this point, the story breaks up:
the wall stutters, incoherent
in a litter of paint flakes.

She records that the presence of the male body
in the text disrupts it.
Here lies, she guesses, Eros:
her hero, naked and unconscious.

Her task is to rescue what she can
from the fresco: not
to smooth-talk; not to make him up.
Woken by her hot look, he sulks. He
never asked for this, resists

her questioning hands, her
fingers pattering at him, white
braille in white dust.

Possibly she's absurd.
Anyway, it is the work that matters.

In the Tradescant garden, Lambeth

In the wings
of the grey church
here in the garden of the dead
the stone box of Tradescant bones
is dark in the rain, under
the gurgle of blackbirds.

Cold bees dive and swerve
by the sweetbriar hedge, by
the blue burn of violets.

Jehane and I, giantesses
in black raincoats
stomp round the
knee-high privet knot
crouch to repeat names
uttered by white tongues:
artemesia, digitalis, saxifrage
stinking hellebore, asphodel.

Doll-sized, we enter
these green loops
a script that writes
that separates
compartments
tight with hyssop
heartsease, thrift.

My two grandmothers
have taken over the church:
the funeral urn pours tea
into green Utility cups.

The Queen's man in his tomb
the scholar, the connoisseur
is a collection of dry sticks
spelling a hexagram of hope: his
dust intact, he spurns
the worms, those fond
greedy under-gardeners.
He seeks promotion to a purer
sphere, a higher court. He'd
change this parterre
for a paradise.

Hester his relict
rots down somewhere else
divorced, mislaid;
her virtues blank
in the carved poem.

Hers is the dirty
alphabet of earth, the
dance of atoms and
of meanings, a
translation
between words not worlds: her
truth is vegetable, her
sex linguistic.

Letting her
self go, letting herself
be worked upon
so that the garden's speech
may be reborn:

this is the undying
labour of the gardener's wife.

The visit

A garden in full flood
brims at the windowsill.
Squares of transparent glass
press back green light, a
green sea, from white walls.

The red
kitchen submarine
carries a cargo of wine and
eggs, fresh cardamom.

Nosing past violent
hedges and grass, the
drip, drip of white
lilac, white roses
we lay out
our card-words.
Kali means *hot*. A
stranger, an angel
dances and burns
on the tip of my tongue.

I sleep in a high bed
pillowed on hills. Clouds
slide in, sidle
over the blue blanket.

In the night, piano music
rises up through the still house
and the silence, grows
like a swift tree
inventing

the tall well
of the spiralling stairs.

Then the cool notes
break and
fall, scatter
white petals in the darkness.

The return

This cathedral is God's
great whorled ear. Under
a roof of giant cockleshells
sung prayers stream
up, shoals of bright fish
flicking through water
over pebbles of stained glass.

This is my father's country
I've entered. This
is my father's house
– the Anglican one – I scorned:
its prim hats
and habits, its
grenadier parsons, its
teapot God.

I'm back, Dad! Your
prodigal daughter
in a shiny black mac
with my battered
heart, my suitcase of poems.

Sssh. There is a wedding
going on here
in a swarm of red
deaconesses
a roar of choirs.

My father leaps up
in the high space
and the mother I thought was lost

ricochets
round him. Strong
arches and vaults of flesh
enclose them. These
two make the sculptured air.
They are the architects. This
design is their dance.

I believe in the big ribbed boat
of the upturned church.
I believe in the body:
the house
the man and woman build
with the sweat of love.

A harvest journey

July was for undoing: I unpicked
my dark blue wedding dress
snipping at it stitch
by sorry stitch. What
to make of it?
Suddenly my hands
opened and my lap
emptied, letting
all those yards of heavy cotton go.

Wet September under Mendip
smelled of hot straw
and cow dung. Yellow
pears, bird-pecked, plummeted
to black earth sprouting
peppery nasturtiums.
The hills left the garden
in one blue fell swoop.

I helped my father pick and chop
apples and onions for chutney
prune the beech tree
with ladder and long shears.
He coughed rough spittle
into his handkerchief. My
mother complained the tall
branches were cruelly
lopped, that Dad's leeks
had wooden hearts. The string beans
quarrelled with the runners, the pot
clanged while the iron hissed.
I cooked omelettes, a sort of blessing.

Ploughs in Devon
stripped the great
valleys' flanks
back to the rich red bone.
Bullocks fattened for the butcher.
My days were bounded by thick strips
of coloured light, curves
of water, of shining rain

the smile and frown
of Dad in his old brown sweater
bringing bowls of spinach
and lettuces in.

Psyche and the hurricane

Freak weather
the forecasters called it, that
the computers couldn't catch.

In the dark single eye
of the storm
dedicated, intent

this island was found
offensive, to be
plucked out.

Some hasty goddess
tossed trees like cabers
tore strips off houses

set electricity loose.
So the white seas rose
to bang the prison-ship

against the rocks
till its belly split, spilt
out the bruised refugees.

I slept through it all in London
woke only to the tinkle
of breaking glass

though in my dreams
wanting letters, wanting
love, I heard her uproar.

From the train I saw the sky fall
onto the flooded
fields, pewter-blue

sun whiten the factory
windows, a hawthorn
burn red and yellow.

The grasses by the slagheaps
bloomed with light:
they were heavy with it.

In Leeds a red-headed woman
taught me a form
of patience, a pagan one:

how to cut coloured bits
from my chaotic
darkness, name and arrange them.

On Monday, in Essex
I counted the local damage:
the beech tree smashed onto the church

porch, the two Scotch firs
crushing the house opposite
the polluted sludge from the estuary

silting up windowsills
the roofs that simply vanished
leaving gaps of flat disbelief.

Wivenhoe Park was choked
by corpses, reclining.
The wind had wrung their necks

dangling and snapped, wrenched
ancient horse-chestnuts' roots
up out of great pits

laid them out, naked and dead
at loggerheads. Then the funerals
began, with fire, the whine of chainsaws.

I have lost Eros. My love
has been ripped
out, leaving me

shaped to this emptiness.
When I remember
his mouth on my breast

that startling current
jumps live again.
I'm un-earthed, I could be

dangerous. The red-headed woman
deals out my tasks. Number
one: face loneliness.

She sends me back to work
on the wind
with her blessing.

You can't
summon an angel.

You can't
force the miraculous light
to slide from the star
and pierce your ear.

You have to give up
expecting it.

The proud girl
available to every
friend, belonging
to no one, she
has to sit
alone in the kitchen's
red stir of silence
admitting her emptiness.

How can this be enough?
All she has to offer:
two open hands
no one might need.

She wants to promise
the one she can't see
she'll attempt to be ready.

A breath on her neck.
Her back, arched like a cat's
tries to jump away.

Why me? she bristles
to the blur of wings:
choose someone else!

Her assent
imprints her with
imagination's truth:

the angel re-enters her.

She watches the coffee-pot
start to shine, the edge
of the sugar bowl jiggle
with life. She carries
her future
carefully
inside herself: the words
she will share
with Elizabeth.

Going into Cornelissen's, Great Russell Street

The window held
jointed wooden
dolls: idols; the
toys of artists; it
drew me in.

The entrance: deep
as the tunnel
leading to that boy-king's
tomb; gilded
box within box, the
high doors
of his outermost skin
guarded by two still jackals
his entrails and heart packed
tight in
alabaster
canopic jars, the
square coffer tenderly braced
by four little
golden goddesses, one
at each corner, their
outstretched arms long as wings
their fingertips
touching each other's.

That moment
when the furthest cave
suddenly becomes a shrine
because the god is there.
I blinked on a blare of colour I
couldn't chew or swallow:

his invisible face
a dazzle of ground paint
incarnate, purely material.

Ranked on the shelves
fat bottles of clear
glass collected the light
separately, and
classified it, like
alphabets, or musical notes:
to render it bearable.

There were jars
transparent with the word *blue*:
turquoise, brilliant and sifted
violet, soft as chiffon
the iridescent pearl salts
of mauve and ultramarine.

Then an ampoule of orange henna
jazzed with saffron
yellow as wet sand
a staff of coffee, of *pain brûlé*
dissolved to contralto
rose, to
a screech of lime sorbet.

Flaring across the shop
the colours and light
burnt onto my retina
the dark of my eyelids
my heart.

Staggering
under the impact of the god
I found all the world
alive, refracted
inside me:
I composed
love's radiance
and held him.

A psalm for Easter
(for Jamila Embarek)

I

This was the night
when the chosen people
journeyed out of Egypt
towards the promised land.

This was the night
when the Red Sea parted
to give them safe passage
out of captivity.

This was the night
when the new fire
burned in the darkness
and the darkness could not extinguish it.

This was the night
when blood was smeared on the doorposts
when the Word burst from the sealed tomb
and out of death delivered us.

II

You gave to me.
You made me remember
my mother

how love
lugged her across the water
and made her strong

how she gave herself up
how she let life rip her
apart, in the name of love

how she gave birth
in a cold foreign town
alone, among strangers

how her son died on the third day
and was buried
and did not rise again.

III

You hung your arms
around our necks.

You slumped between us
your head on Pat's breast

and then on mine.
We held you up

on the edge of the metal bed.
We were your witnesses.

How you laboured
night into day into night

how dolorously
the delivery room

contracted to
pains that skewered you.

You thirsted. We laid
our wet fingers against your lips.

You clutched our hands
and didn't let go:

you cried out in Arabic and French
your mother-tongue, and mine

sometimes for your mother
and sometimes for me.

You doubted. You disbelieved.
You called for a knife

to cut you, quickly:
my husband, my husband

why have you abandoned me?
At the end, you abandoned yourself:

you put yourself to death.
You delivered yourself up:

then your son flashed out
like a fish, across the green sheet.

You turned your head away.
It was finished.

IV

This was the night
outside the hospital
when the milkman's cart
clattered in the frosty street.

This was the night
when four men in white walked past us
lighting the dark suburb
with four bright candle flames.

This was the night
the full moon hung above us
low and heavy as your breast
dented like your baby's head.

This was the night
I dreamed of a derelict old woman
her sodden nappy of newspapers
interleaved with poems.

This was the night
I learned the weight of sorrow
the weight of the sad body
my hands could hold.

V

They hung you, my daughter
on a metal cross.

From your precious wound
your blood fell out

thickly, collected in a bucket.
The green-gowned Sister

sat between your legs.
Where she had cut you

64

she stitched you up.
She wove you back together

with black threads. With her needle
she repaired the damage.

Then we unstrapped you
and took you down.

Then we laid you
unconscious, to rest.

VI

You gave to me.
You made me remember
my mother

and how I mourned, being born
alive, being born a daughter
how I thought I broke her, being born

how I wanted to break her again
and make her mourn
how I too was broken

how I was Egypt, that sad land
how I was the sealed tomb
with dead words inside.

You made me remember
how the mother must mourn the lost son
how the daughters must mourn

the lost mother, must ask
for forgiveness, how the daughters
must find and tend

the broken body of love
must mend it, must make
reparation.

VII

On the morning of the third day
love rose up early
inside the tomb.

Love breathed in my ear
and lifted me.
Love set me upright.

Then love rolled the stone away.
Then love opened my mouth.
Then love made me rise.

And I, who had died in this life
was born back into it.
I, who had died, was risen.

And she whom I had been searching for
was there. She was with me.
She was love's body:

alive
made whole again
in me.

Tourists on Grisedale Pike

The mountain held
one small
wall of ice in its
green valley, a deep stream
in its tense fold
where boys in blue kagouls
larked and picnicked.

We knuckled up
the stony spine of
this bit of planet.
Slopes fell away till
our eyes levelled
with distant snows
and other mountains
plunged, sprawled
tipsily below us.

You sat back, happy
on the tilt of rock
solid, sharing whisky and
dolcelatte sandwiches, feet
braced over nothingness.

I feared the wind would
whirl me off
into the drop of
air, that loose
spiralling cone
of the mountain
turned upside down:
I wanted to fly

to let go and fall
from our great height
into Derwentwater.

I tested *vertiginous*
on your mouth's
taste of garlic and olives
and held on
to the view of no lack
all the way down:

the graphite mine
sinking its rusty teeth
in the valley's side
geese plumping up nicely
in orchards, the kestrels
choosing their prey, poised over
the fat mound of Swinside Hill.

Early morning
in the farmhouse near Keswick
we climbed each other again
under the stolid glare
of our landlady's
many sepia babies.
Late down to breakfast:
Mrs Cook ticked us off
for our *hectic nights.*

Cockermouth too
the local paper warned
would soon be corrupted.

On Criffel

The mountain's
bottom was a black sponge
squeezed between raw forests.
It slurped as we pressed it
under our boots
our legs lifting
steeply through peat bogs

so water sprang, seeped
mixed us into moist air, cut
shelves of fibrous earth
shoulder after shoulder
of scratchy furze.

Worth it, on top
for the flat map
of lochs and pink fields
the edge of Scotland
pushed in and out
by the flood of the sea.

Here we rescued a dog in distress
the silk-bellied dachshund
lost, who had followed us up.
Calmly she flopped
a plump parcel awaiting collection.
We plopped her into your rucksack
head lolling over the edge
for a placid view
then slipped and skidded down
the soft hills, you muttering
insults and threats

in gangster accents
to kidnapped canines
lest you be thought
some fucking St Francis
or worse still, heroic.

I trotted behind, supplying
sotto voce endearments
to both of you.

Man pregnant with dog.
I loved you so much
I kept falling over.

In the New Year

A green tree in the dark house.
Hard buds of coloured light
stripped off it
at Epiphany, the
solid coffin
of the lopped spruce
carted out
by two of us, dumped
onto gravel.

Fourteen children
lay on the hill holding hands
in a ring
under a streak of stars
wishing for
one pulse, one
red dawn body.

The leaving train
tracked Devon's lip
licked and
bitten by sea.
As the sun jumped up
the silk of the mud flats
was amethyst
the world suddenly flushed
fat with radiance.

It all heaved up in me:
love, sobs, knowledge

the closeness of hedges and grass
how the one body was both of us.

In London
cold beads of water
marbled the indigo glass night.
The hyacinths
unclenched blue fists.
You delved in, rooting
me till
our dark body sparked with light.

The announcement was made in mud:
sticky river of mud, slither
of bluebells down hidden
hills in the woods.

Some buds were downy
and thick as lips.
Some were tight
spindles in pale pink
satiny wraps.
Some began to unfurl
delicate   wet
caterpillars dangling trans-
parently in green light.

In the snailshell
of the secret church
she listened for a heartbeat's
echo on
white walls
the packed brick floor.

Showers of ice and sun
swept through the great meadow's
turbulent grass.
The flowers
fastened in the bare
black hawthorn tree
broke loose
and shouted out.
Rejoice. Rejoice.

White stars flung themselves
to the ground. Onto
her knees she went amongst
anemones, celandines. Her
heart unclosed its lips
and sang this song.

Silver outlined the far sheep
on the valley side
kindled the darkness
of tufts of grass. Each
blue cabbage
in the glittering field
was a crisp world of light.

The day the wall came down

1

We began as one
pram with two hoods
a secret language
a single dent in the bed.

At eleven plus
we failed at arithmetic
simple division
the test of love.

I thought you'd got all the heart
that I'd gobbled your brain.

To keep myself in
I had to keep you out:
our free air
hardened to glass
unscratchable.

The times were un-nourishing.
There was one too many:
it was you or me.

You thinned yourself
down to bone
broth. Your hair fell out.
Your toes and fingers turned blue.
I was white fat, pork belly
I was mash and grease.

Both of us
made ourselves scarce.
Our conjuring trick:
our disappearing needs.

Sometimes, from far away
I'd holler
into your silence, at
our sad milk.

2

Our date: astonishing November
near Euston
an oven-basement
where lunch
eats up the afternoon

and we chew over
the babies you've got
the baby I dreamed I'd steal

and you feed me advice fresh
and gritty as pepper, necessary
as salt

my sister in black and silver
your breath close, your
face flushed with wine

and we taste garlic, spaghetti
anchovies, broccoli
hot with red chillies

and what has divided us
comes down

the work of our mouths
desirous
eating, meeting.

3

Twins with our guards
torn down: now
we reclaim
each other's hidden city
as our own, the
other side of skin.

Foreign as freedom
on my new route back

to slip on the silvery
grease of pavements
smell the secret life of Camden
feel the electric blue
bruise of the evening sky
over the railway lines
of Kentish Town

where cafés offer honeycakes
the tick of dominoes
contact with strangers'
eyes idling by TV screens

and greengrocers' caves
are dark mouths, bearded
with cloths of grass
moustached by swags of brilliant
bulbs, pearl onions.

In my arms rustle papery
sheaths: inky irises

unfurl their blue fur tongues
anemones in mud-coloured ruffs
open their fat black eyes
a shout of purple.

All the way home
I listen to
the morse code of
woodpeckers

my sister calling for
me through the cold
years, the

tapping
of the axes
of love.

4

The pour of bodies.
The gap.

Memorial
to that which is still missing
all that which longs to be said.

The diagnosis

Not two years' age
difference. Not
politics. What
separates us now:

your pain

I can't take
from you or
hold. Not
a crying child
who could be comforted.

I sit with it
witness it

want to sort it out:
colours for
cold, hot washes.
Not to be folded
smoothed, and put away.

Grief was a pharmacist.
Now grief wears a blue
cotton sunhat
and is hairless.

Another leak
in the lavatory roof
drip drip down the lightbulb.
I pissed in the dark, raindrops
smacking my shoulder-blades.

This morning I woke
to fresh wet birdsong
under a cloud of quilt
last night's hot sweetness
still fizzing between my legs.

I was fooled into swallowing spring
jumping up to make tea
and rinse dishes, whistle
a liquid kitchen oratorio.

It's your birthday next week.
This time next year
I think you'll be gone
quietly as this water
slipping over my hands.

After your funeral
we'll return
to your parched house.
We'll try to hold our mother up
like this exhausted roof.

I carry your dying
inside me
as real as milk

as I'll carry on
getting the roof fixed
making love
weeping into the washing-up.

A walk on the south downs

In January
even the wind is lean
trimming the hawthorns
to blunt, bent doggedness

scraping the downs
out; hollow
vistas of hunger
a morphine fast.

Your body is
a die that
stamps
these hills: the stretch
of your pain
repeatedly
struck into soft chalk.

Jim and I
flounder up
valleys of mud
bulky as elephants
clotting our boots

winter slapping loose
lips together: mud
swallows, mud belch.

So easy, in this tired air
to let go your hand
the hedgerows' whippy support
yield, slide
to that sucking bed

not to plod on, haul
our legs
to the top
of the tunnelling path

tip ourselves out
over the gate
onto sheep-nibbled
tumbledown slopes

where the long man
rests, the
sunset under his feet
his outline restored in white chalk
his empty belly full of fresh grass.

mayday mayday

The fields here tick over
with dandelion clocks
fragile and full
as luminous as moons.

Your room smells of fish and shit.
You curl in your nightie
a clack of bones.
Your guts are plastic
gartered to your thin thigh.

Down the lane the maypole
shakes out its ribbons
on pointed toes.
Solemn and quick
the children's knees skip up.
Sandals and anoraks.
Print frocks as
sharp as lettuces. Your
death dances forwards. Your
death dances back.

I do what I can:
bleed the fridge dry
hack up the chicken for soup
rip milky weeds from the grass.

You thrash on.
Death's hooks in
your belly, your mouth.

You're so pale. Parched
as these London streets
cracking up in the heat.

The butcher's in Holloway Road
gusts forth the smell of warm blood.

Your voice on the telephone
stumbles: so far away.

I slept in your attic
looking over the long hill.
The open window let in
cold sweet darkness
impersonal stars
sheep crying in the night.

home alterations

You were their safe house.

Aged forty-three
you vanish.

In your place
a tiny wizened crone
flat as the sheets.

Changeling. Bone
puppet with bright
monkey eyes. Your
leather paw
dangles in mine.

Your seams keep coming unstitched.
Your stuffing
shoves itself out.

A thimble of water.
A postage-stamp of toast.

The bedroom jumps and shudders.
You fight and vomit
listen to
death
drill through the wall

death in his vest
death with his metal
elbow, his
yellow metal claw.

Your kitchen's gone
torn off like an arm
chewed up then
spat out in concrete.
Death whistles
stripping you down
to your foundations.

From the top of the hill
I look back, watch
you shrink into
your child's dolls house

hear you slam shut
your splintering door
against big baby death's
needy touches and greedy reach.

Midsummer's Day.
The darkest.
Red growls of poppies.
Skies in the afternoon
blacken like spoiled wheat.

A clutch of women
in the kitchen mixes
tears and
shoulders, the remains
of a hot roast dinner.

You're a skull on the pillows
two hands that
jerk and grope
in receding air
to the pulse of the drug-
pump, a
mutter: *it's so strange.*

I kiss your soft blistered lips.
Leaving.
Trying to let go.
I blurt out: *you won't
kick the bucket just yet.*
You smile at me:
oh yes I think I will.

Our mother stays with you.
Must watch

day by day
your life torn off
you, red
poppy petals.

for Jackie

We're back
in the old
house, the one on cine-film:
Dad in his shirt-sleeves
grinning, Mum
with her hair pinned up
her short fur jacket.

You haven't left.
And now
there's a verandah
at the front:
half-in, half-out
your bed of glass.

You sit up, lively.
Arms outstretched.
In conversation.
What joy, sister
to see you lucid.

Uncles and aunts and cousins
fill up the room behind.
A sort of party.
I'm expecting twins.

I wake in my own
bed. Thirsty.
I haven't slept.
Dreaming about you all night.

Cold water in a cup.
The kitchen glimmers. Gold
sucks me up
feet on a chair, headfirst
through the attic skylight.
Dawn breaks like red glass.

The phonecall comes at seven.

You died in your sleep
as the day began.

He arrives too early
the back of his lorry
stacked with black booty.

A mask and gloves of soot.
Ten menacing sacks
lounge on the path.
He says he's been ordered
to shoulder these bully-boys in.

Already
he's taken the lid off
the coal cellar's mouth
by the front steps.

I stumble underground.
Start shovelling.

Daylight's round eye
level with mine
is blacked
out. Coal's relentless fists
pummel the earth floor.
Knobbles of darkness
roar past my knees
in a rubble tide.

Forced food of
dust. The cellar chokes.

A loose black hill
collapses in my house.
Black landslide

cold as the torrent
bearing you along

my sister
in a long box

to be burnt up
swallowed into black ash.

You're outside
the Father's house
in God's backyard. Packed
litter of stone
beds and lids, tall
granite doors.

Charlotte could not forget
the dying Emily
turning her eyes
reluctantly
from the pleasant sun

You're still my sister.
You reappear: your
scrawl on
my birthday card
my scribbled time-
table of trains
departing from Paddington
the visiting hours
the hospital's address.

Waking, I think
sleeping, I dream of her
still she appears to me
in sickness and suffering

You've been
ground by the fire
to powder, your
round flesh

compacted
to a cube of dust.

I remembered where she was laid
in what narrow dark dwelling.
So the sense of desolation
took possession of me

Earth tightens around you
little box. Safe now
swaddled with flowers.

Now I sit by myself.
Necessarily I am silent.

In branches of Culpepper
they lie in baskets:
long, dark and wrinkled.

Proper cooks
keep a pod in the sugar
to imbue their cakes
with a sweet, aromatic flavour.

Vanilla planifolia, a
lusty member of the orchid
family, climbs & creeps.
Beans, to people
in the spice business.

In Madagascar, the vines
are trained up small trees
known as *tuteurs*. On
the islands of the Camores
Mayotte & Reunion
vanilla is grown
in the sugar-cane fields.

Vanilla flowers
are hand-pollinated
by *fécondeuses*:
women & children
whose task it is
to pass between the vines
daily, for several months.

The mis-leading nature
of food-labelling legislation
does little to improve
the plight of genuine vanilla.

The word *vanilla* has become
a 'customary term':
to many people
vanilla simply means
plain, uncoloured.

'Put it like this'
the icecream salesman said:
'ours isn't natural from the seedpod.'

'Is vanilla a country?'
asked my neighbour:
'a hot, wet island
east of Africa?'

Exported by vanilla barons
in metal boxes
lined with greaseproof paper
(untold quantities also go
into Coca-Cola)

chastely wrapped in cellophane
priced £1.25 apiece.

(Words taken from a *Guardian* article on vanilla by Alexandra Buxton, May 1990)

In Julie's house
coloured lavender, lemon, pink

black-browed madonnas
lounge on chaise-longues

next to buddhas
sharing cigars
with cooks and anarchists.

An ebony vase
tips out a riff of orange tulips

armchairs in Chinese shawls
jiggle their silvery fringed hips

a black tin tray
drums patterns of red
poppies, anemones

and bread jumps up in the oven
spinach in the back plot
to sambas, to salsa.

High-shouldered ducks
limbo past to the pond.

The cold taste
of mountain air.
The perfume of coffee
picked in Nicaragua. Her
talk tangy as margaritas.

A gypsy house
that pauses against this hill.
Its doors disclose twin
stairs, a secret
corridor, high
beds for lovers.

It is Easter morning.
A gold brocaded egg
cracks open
in the dark kitchen.